To the reader:

Welcome to the DK ELT Graded Readers! These readers are
different. They explore aspects of the world around us: its history,
geography, science … and a lot of other things. And
they show the different ways in which people live now, and
lived in the past.

These DK ELT Graded Readers give you material for reading
for information, and reading for pleasure. You are using your
English to do something real. The illustrations will help you
understand the text, and also help bring the Reader to life.
There is a glossary to help you understand the special words for
this topic. Listen to the cassette or CD as well, and you can
really enter the world of the Olympic Games, the *Titanic*, or the
Trojan War … and a lot more. Choose the topics that interest
you, improve your English, and learn something … all at the
same time.
Enjoy the series!

To the teacher:

This series provides varied reading practice at five
levels of language difficulty, from elementary to
FCE level:
BEGINNER
ELEMENTARY A
ELEMENTARY B
INTERMEDIATE
UPPER INTERMEDIATE
The language syllabus has been
designed to suit the factual
nature of the series, and includes
a wider vocabulary range than is usual
with ELT readers: language linked
with the specific theme of each book
is included and glossed. The language
scheme, and ideas for exploiting the
material (including the recorded
material) both in and out of class are
contained in the Teacher's Resource Book.
We hope you and your students enjoy using
this series.

Dorling **DK** Kindersley

LONDON, NEW YORK, SYDNEY, DELHI,
PARIS, MUNICH & JOHANNESBURG

Originally published as Dorling Kindersley
Reader *Spooky Spinechillers* in 2000, text
© Andrew Donkin, and adapted as an ELT
Graded Reader for Dorling Kindersley by

studio **cactus** ©

13 SOUTHGATE STREET WINCHESTER HAMPSHIRE SO23 9DZ

Published in Great Britain by
Dorling Kindersley Limited
9 Henrietta Street, London WC2E 8PS

2 4 6 8 10 9 7 5 3 1

Copyright © 2000
Dorling Kindersley Limited, London

A CIP catalogue record for this book is
available from the British Library.

ISBN 0-7513-2944-4

Colour reproduction by Colourscan, Singapore
Printed and bound in China by
L. Rex Printing Co., Ltd
Text film output by Chimera.trt, UK

The publisher would like to thank the following
for their kind permission to reproduce their photographs:
c=centre; t=top; b=below; l=left; r=right

AKG London: 20; Fortean Picture Library: 17cr, 24tl,
28tl, 44tl; Harry Price Collection, University of London:
5, 22–23, 23tr; Hulton Getty: 11tr, 38clb; Katz Pictures:
34clb; Mary Evans Picture Library: 7tr, 18–19, 19tr, 19br,
21tr, 22tl, 22clb, 30bl, 36tl, 41tr, 43tr, 44–45, 46; Peter
Underwood: 24cl, 24–25, 26; Quadrant Picture Library:
Slick Shoots 12tl; Robert Harding Picture Library:
Michael Short 6tl; Robert Francis 32tl; South American
Pictures: Charlotte Lipson 47cr; Tibet Images: Ian
Cumming 28clb; Tony Stone Images: Tony Craddock 18cl

See our complete catalogue at
www.dk.com

Contents

ELT Graded Readers

INTERMEDIATE

GHOSTS

Written by David Maule

Series Editor Susan Holden

A Dorling Kindersley Book

Halloween
The traditional time for ghosts to walk the Earth is Halloween, on 31 October. That's when the wall between the living and the dead is said to be easiest to pass through.

Old haunts
The earliest recorded haunted house was in Greece, 2,000 years ago. A ghostly figure drove away people living in a house in Athens.

Ghosts and spirits

It's nearly midnight. You're completely lost, far from the nearest town. And now it has started to rain. You come to a large old house. Maybe the people will let you stay the night there, or at least tell you where you are. There are no lights on. You don't want to wake anybody up, but you're cold and wet. So you knock on the large wooden door.

Nobody answers. You knock again. Maybe the house is empty. You turn the handle and … the door opens.

You stand for a moment, staring into the darkness. Then you switch on your torch and walk along the cold empty hall.

This is how we might imagine a ghost story would begin. In fact, when you read the stories in this book, you will find that many people saw ghosts in very ordinary situations – on a plane, for example, or in a modern kitchen.

And that, perhaps, is the most frightening thing of all. Ghosts, it seems, can be anywhere, and appear to anyone. As you read this book, you will realize just how true this can be. And then you might find yourself looking over your shoulder just a little more often.

A photo of the ghost of Raynham Hall, Norfolk, England.

The next victim

Castle ghosts
Ireland is full of old castles. It is said that Leap Castle, near Munster, has many ghosts. These include an animal-man – with a horrible smell.

Top haunts
Ireland has a long tradition of being one of the most haunted places in the world.

Arthur Frewen was lost. The 20-year-old student was on holiday on the south-east coast of Ireland. He was staying with friends in Dungarvan, in County Waterford. He had been for a walk, but he couldn't find his way back. And now it was getting dark.

Arthur stopped and looked around. He was walking along a path near the sea and he didn't know whether it was taking him nearer the town or further away. But it was quite cold now, and even going in the wrong direction was better than standing still.

Arthur wrapped his red scarf around his neck and moved on. Soon, it was dark, but he could just see his way by the moonlight. Then, he came around the side of some rocks, and saw a light ahead.

As he came closer, he saw that the light came from a fishing boat. There was somebody on the deck. Arthur walked towards him, and soon saw that this was quite an old man. He was mending a fishing net. Arthur explained that he was lost, and the man invited him to come onto the boat.

Irish ghost
A banshee is a traditional form of Irish ghost. Some people have heard its horrible cries just before a death.

"Are you hungry?"

Arthur said that he was. He followed the fisherman down into the boat's kitchen. There was a pot of hot soup on the cooker, with steam rising from it. Arthur watched as the old man filled a bowl, then sat down and began to eat.

The man said nothing, but stood and watched him steadily. This made Arthur feel quite uncomfortable, and he ate the soup as quickly as possible.

"Come this way," the man said, as soon as Arthur finished. He led the way to a small cabin. Arthur said thank you and watched as the man moved back to the kitchen. Then he closed the door firmly and hung his scarf on the back of it. He looked around. There was one small window, but no pictures or anything else on the walls. He climbed into the bed and closed his eyes. He was tired, but each time he fell asleep, he woke up suddenly because he could hear the man sharpening a knife.

Just after midnight, Arthur woke again. This time, he heard footsteps coming towards his door. He got out of the bed and looked through the keyhole. There, walking towards him, was the old man. In his hand, he held a large knife. Arthur turned and pushed the window open. The handle of the cabin door was beginning to turn, but he managed to pull himself through the window.

Arthur hid for the rest of the night. He found his way back to Dungarvan early the next morning.

Arthur told his friends what had
happened, and they decided to go back to
the boat together. But, when they got to
the beach, there was only an old boat
with many holes in its sides.

"Perhaps you met the Dungarvan
murderer," one of his friends said,
laughing. "This is supposed to be his
boat. He invited people onto it, then
killed them with a big knife. The police
caught him in the end."

"So he escaped from prison …"
Arthur said. "We should call the police."

"It's too late for that," his friend said.
"They hanged him in Dungarvan more
than 70 years ago. The last person he
killed was a student, just like you."

Arthur felt his hands turning cold, and he began to shake a little. None of this made sense. He pushed his way through a hole in the boat's side. The wood was wet and turning green and he had to cover his nose to keep out the smell. But it looked like the same boat, and he even found a cabin like the one he had slept in. He spoke to one of his friends through a hole in the wall.

"It looks very similar," he said, "only older."

"Don't be silly," his friend said. "Fishing boats are all much the same. Maybe it came from the same builder. You had a bad dream, that's all."

"Yes," Arthur said. "You're probably right."

He turned to leave, and stopped dead, his eyes widening. His red scarf was hanging on the back of the cabin door.

Attractions
Public hangings often attracted a large crowd. The victims often made a last speech to the crowd before they were hanged.

Ghost cat
In 1968, the ghost of a cat appeared several times to workmen in a house in southern Ireland. The animal was as big as a dog. It terrified all the men with its red and orange eyes.

11

The crew of ghosts

L-1011
A Lockheed
L-1011 aeroplane
is also known as a
Tristar airbus.

It was 23.34 on 29 December, 1972. A Lockheed Tristar belonging to Eastern Airlines was getting close to Miami. The voice of the plane's captain, Bob Loft, was heard in the control tower. "This is Eastern 401. It looks like we're going to have to circle." There was a small light on the plane that usually showed that the nose wheel was down. This light hadn't come on. There was a problem.

While the first officer tried to check the lightbulb, the flight engineer, Don Repo, went to see if he could get a look at the nose wheel. Bob Loft took the plane up to 600 metres and switched on the automatic pilot.

Bad news
The crash of
Flight 401 was
reported all over
the world.

But the first officer couldn't get the lightbulb out of the panel. The captain got out of his seat to help – and as he did so, he knocked against a switch and turned off the automatic pilot. The plane began to drop slowly towards the ground.

At 23.42, the first officer asked if the plane was still at 600 metres. Bob Loft's last words, in this world at least, were, "Hey, what's happening here?" Three seconds later the plane hit the ground. One hundred people, including Bob Loft and Don Repo, died.

Flying time
The plane used during Flight 401 had completed a total of nearly 1,000 hours in the air and more than 500 safe landings.

Early warning
Doris Elliot, a crew member with Eastern Airlines, dreamed about the crash a month before it happened. She saw a plane crashing at night in the Everglades. She even told people the week it would happen.

About three months after the crash, a high-level manager of Eastern Airlines was flying to Miami. He sat down beside a man in captain's uniform in the first-class area. He couldn't quite place the man's face in his mind. They spoke for a few minutes, and then the manager realized that he was talking to Bob Loft. Suddenly, the captain disappeared.

A week later, an Eastern Airlines captain and two of his crew went into a crew room at John F. Kennedy Airport in New York. All of them saw Bob Loft sitting alone in a chair. He talked to them for a while, then disappeared. The men were so shocked they had to cancel their flight.

Three weeks later, a woman was sitting in the first-class cabin of a flight to Miami. She was worried about the man in an Eastern Airlines uniform next to her. His face was white and he looked ill, so she called over a stewardess and asked her to help him.

The stewardess leaned over to speak to the man, but he ignored her. Then, he slowly disappeared.

The stewardess was deeply shocked, and she was taken to hospital in Miami. Later, she was shown some photographs. When she saw Don Repo's picture, she recognized the man she had seen.

Things didn't stop there: the strange appearances continued.

Seen by many
There have been more recorded sightings of the ghosts of Flight 401 than of any other ghost.

Safe travel
In the USA, fewer people have died in air crashes in the past 60 years than die in car accidents in a typical three-week period.

Ghost flier
Visitors and workers at the Castle Air Force Museum in California, USA, have seen the ghost of another pilot. It haunts the cabin of a World War II aeroplane on show there.

Over the next few months, more than ten people working for Eastern Airlines said they had seen Don Repo. On one occasion, he appeared to men who were putting food onto an aeroplane. They dropped everything and ran away in terror. They knew he was dead.

It seemed that his intentions were sometimes good, however, because on another occasion he warned a crew to watch out for fire on their plane. A fire did break out on that flight, but the crew was ready for it and put it out quickly.

After the crash of Flight 401, all the parts of the aeroplane that were not damaged were taken away and kept by the company. These had to be tested, of course, but if they were safe, there was no reason why they could not be used again. So, in the months after the crash, they were put into some other Eastern Airlines planes. Then somebody wondered if, perhaps, Don Repo appeared only on planes carrying parts from Flight 401. When this idea was checked, it turned out to be true.

Some people have doubted the whole story of the ghosts of Flight 401. They have said that people were imagining things, or perhaps passing on what they'd heard. However, the fact is that Eastern Airlines took the "parts" idea very seriously. They ordered their mechanics to take out everything from Flight 401 from their other planes. A number of expensive items were taken out and thrown away.

And it seemed to work. After that, Bob Loft and Don Repo left Eastern Airlines and their planes in peace.

Airport ghost
A man in a black hat haunts Heathrow Airport in London. He stands on the spot where his plane crashed in 1948.

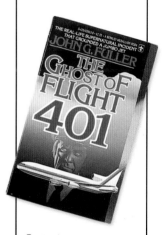

In print
The journalist John Fuller studied the ghosts of Flight 401. He spoke to many people who said they had seen one. He wrote a best-selling book that told the story.

Adventure
Ann Moberly and Eleanor Jourdain wrote a book about their walk in Versailles. It was called *An Adventure* and appeared in 1911.

A walk in the past

It was 10 August, 1901. Ann Moberly and Eleanor Jourdain, two Englishwomen, were on holiday in Paris. That day, they visited the Palace of Versailles. At about four o'clock in the afternoon, they decided to visit a house in the gardens known as the Petit Trianon. This is quite a long way from the main palace.

French palace
The French king Louis XIV started to build the Palace of Versailles in 1661, in the place where a smaller royal house had stood. It was finished in 1756.

The two women were not very sure how to get there. Also, their minds were far away, talking about friends in England. They soon became lost.

They saw two men. There were some gardening tools near them, but they didn't look like gardeners. They were both very well dressed in long, greyish-green coats and old-fashioned three-cornered hats. The women stopped and asked them the way and were told to walk straight on. As they did so, Ann began to feel that something was wrong.

They crossed a small bridge over a stream and the Petit Trianon came into sight.

Royal gift
The Petit Trianon was built in 1763. Louis XVI gave it to his wife, Marie Antoinette, when he became king in 1774.

Horse and cart
When Elizabeth Hatton visited the Palace of Versailles in 1948, she saw an old-style horse and cart that suddenly vanished.

On the grass in front of it, a woman was sitting on a small seat. Ann thought she might be a tourist, except that, as she later wrote, "her dress was old-fashioned and rather unusual". The women walked past her, visited the Petit Trianon and went back to Paris.

Marie Antoinette in the Trianon park, *a painting by Antoine Vestier.*

A week later, Ann was thinking about the visit. Suddenly, she asked her friend "Do you think that the Petit Trianon is haunted?"

"Yes, I do." Eleanor replied immediately.

They talked about the visit, but not very seriously. Three months later, Eleanor came to visit Ann at her home in Oxford. While she was there, Ann mentioned the woman sitting on the seat. Eleanor was surprised and insisted she hadn't seen her. They then decided that each of them should write down her memories of the visit.

The women later discovered that nobody working at Versailles in 1901 wore grey-green coats and three-cornered hats. But, the soldiers who guarded Marie Antoinette had worn uniforms like this.

Three years later, the two women visited the Petit Trianon again, and everything seemed different. The paths were in different places and the bridge that they had crossed didn't exist. However, it was shown on an old map in exactly the position they had described. And this map was found, hidden up a chimney, only in 1903 – two years after the women's first visit.

Revolution
Between 1789 and 1795, a revolution took place in France. Louis XVI and Marie Antoinette were killed and France became a republic.

Into the past
In 1916, Edith Oliver walked around a fairground in the small English village of Avebury. She later discovered that the last fair had been held there in 1850.

Poltergeists
These ghosts cannot be seen. They often throw things violently around a room.

Supernatural
The Foysters were the third family to live in Borley Rectory. All of them experienced strange and frightening things.

Ghosthunter

Strange things were happening in Borley Rectory in England. Whispering voices came from the walls. Footsteps were heard when nobody was there. Lights turned on in empty rooms. Keys disappeared and stones were thrown. Two servants working in the house saw the ghostly figure of a nun. Even an old-fashioned ghostly coach and horses was seen. Guy Smith, a Church of England vicar, had lived at Borley with his wife for less than nine months, and now they needed help. They contacted a national newspaper, the *Daily Mirror*, and discussed the problem.

On 12 June, 1929, a ghosthunter called Harry Price and a *Mirror* reporter arrived at the rectory. On that first visit, they both saw things move for no reason. They noticed strange smells and heard the sound of running horses. They also found places in the house where the temperature was unnaturally low.

It was certainly enough for Price to take the matter seriously. He returned with his ghost-hunting equipment and laid it out in the study. He set up various cameras. He arranged alarms that would go off if anything moved near them while he was asleep. Then he put tape around the door, spread white dust on the floor to show footprints and put a bowl of water on the table to show movement.

But none of this stopped somebody – or something – from locking the study door from inside without Price noticing.

No tricks
Before Harry Price started work on a house, he made sure he knew where everyone was. He often locked people in a room and put tape around the door. This was so that nobody could play tricks on him.

23

Ghost writing
Writing often appeared on the walls of the rectory. It seemed that a ghost wanted to contact the Reverend Foyster's wife, Marianne.

Church ghosts
Nearby Borley Church is also supposed to be haunted. Villagers have heard ghostly footsteps. They have also heard music when the church was empty.

Within a year, the Smiths had left Borley. When the new vicar, Lionel Foyster, moved in, the strange events continued. During the five years that the Foysters lived in Borley Rectory, Harry Price said that at least 2,000 unexplained events took place – although some people said that he had imagined many of them.

In 1935, the Foysters left, not because of the ghosts but because Lionel's bad health meant that he could not continue with his work as a vicar. The church then decided that Borley was unsuitable for vicars to live in. In June 1937, Harry Price moved into the building and advertised for helpers who were willing to spend nights there. They did a number of experiments, but the activity seemed to die down during this period. No ghosts were seen – not even the nun who had appeared so many times.

Price discovered that, although the rectory dated back only to the 1860s, a monastery had once stood in the same place. In 1362, a monk and a nun, from a nearby nunnery, had fallen in love.

They had tried to run away together in a coach, but were caught. The monk was hanged, but the nun's punishment was much worse. She was put into a room, a wall was built across the door, and she was left to starve to death.

Price decided to try to contact the ghosts himself. He used a planchette – a small, heart-shaped board on wheels with a pencil pushed through it. He placed it on a sheet of paper, rested his hand on it, and waited.

Long tradition
Borley Rectory was built by the Reverend Henry Bull in the 1860s, on the spot where another house once stood. This house was there as long ago as 1066. The building later became a monastery.

Borley ghosts
Among the ghosts of Borley Rectory are a large dog and a coach pulled by black horses.

After a while, the planchette began to move. The writing said that the rectory would burn down that very night, and that the body of a nun would be found underneath it. In fact, the house didn't catch fire, or at least not that night.

After Harry Price moved out, the rectory was bought by a man who owned a large number of buildings in the area. He moved there with his two sons.

On 27 February, 1939, while he was sorting out some books at the foot of the main stair, the oil lamp fell over. Very quickly, the whole house caught fire. The fire brigade managed to save some parts of the building, but most of it was destroyed.

Harry Price was still interested in the story of the nun. Four years later, he returned, and began to dig inside the house. After digging down some distance, he found the jawbone of a young woman. Since it wasn't normal to bury bodies within the monastery, he felt it had to be that of the nun.

Harry arranged for the bone to be buried close to the church. In the following year, 1944, the ruins of Borley Rectory were pulled down. Nothing is there now, although there are still reports that the ghost of a nun is seen nearby.

Flaming ghosts
Small flames are sometimes seen in wet areas. They are caused by burning gases from dead plants. People used to think that these were ghosts.

Power of the mind
Monks in Tibet believe they can make a ghost appear by thinking hard. The ghosts are called tulpas and can be good or bad.

Flames of the dead

It was a hot night in June, 1907. Peter Smith, an army officer, was asleep in his house in Delhi, India. Suddenly, he woke up. He sat up in bed and looked at his watch. It was 2.30 a.m. On the wall around his bed he could see flames, and his first thought was that the house was on fire. But the night was silent, and he could smell no smoke. The fire had to be outside. So who was building fires at this time of the night?

He got up and walked across to the window. The garden outside was empty. There was no sign of any fire. He turned and looked back at the dancing flames on the wall. In his time in India, Smith had seen one or two things that were difficult to explain, but this was more strange. He thought about going to one of the nearby houses and calling in another officer, but he didn't really know what he could say. Also, he was tired and it was the middle of the night. He shook his head and went back to bed. Mysteries could wait till the morning. He opened his eyes once more: the flames were still there. Then he fell asleep.

The following night, Smith woke up at exactly the same time. Once again, he could see flames on the wall. He tried to put them out of his mind, and went back to sleep. The same thing happened on the third night. On the fourth night, the flames were larger than ever, and he could hear the sounds of a fire outside. Although it was another hot night, he was shaking a little as he got up and went over to the window.

Protection
Many people in India believe that ghosts are bad and dangerous. Some people build piles of small stones and place food and drink inside for the ghosts. They hope the ghosts will then leave them alone.

29

Yearly ghosts
Some ghosts
appear only on
a certain day each
year. US President
Lincoln was
murdered in 1865.
The ghost of the
train that took
his body home is
often seen on
the same day as
he died.

Smith stared in disbelief. Somebody had built a large fire in his garden. He could see two soldiers, and they were pulling something towards it. Suddenly angry, he threw open the shutters and stepped outside. He took a few steps forwards, then the soldiers and the fire disappeared. He was left standing in an empty garden.

Smith didn't sleep at all well for the rest of that night. He knew he had to speak to somebody about it. He chose an officer who he knew quite well, and told him the whole story. The man listened, his face serious, nodding now and again.

"What you saw sounds like something that happened here 50 years ago," he said. "I heard the story not long after I arrived. There used to be another house, just next door to yours.

The commanding officer and his wife lived there. One night, two officers broke in and murdered both of them. Then they took the bodies outside and pulled them across the garden."

The officer sat back a little in his seat and looked at Smith. "They burned the bodies just outside your window. It happened on a hot night in June."

Ghostbusters
In India, if a family is worried by a bad ghost, they may pay a person called a shaycana to come and frighten it away.

The uninvited guest

Hilary Spence was from Las Vegas, USA. When she returned there from a holiday in England, she took with her a present from her aunt. It was a small house made of china. It had been in her aunt's family for years. Her aunt had kept postage stamps in it. Hilary decided to keep stamps in it, too. She found some in a drawer and put them inside.

After a few days, Hilary began to notice that something was changing in the house. She thought she could see dark shadows moving around the room. It was very difficult to be sure. Also, areas of the kitchen suddenly became very cold.

One night, Hilary was clearing up the kitchen when, out of the corner of her eye, she saw something move. She stood totally still for a moment, feeling her body freeze with fear. She wanted to run away, but the door was on the far side of the kitchen. Terrified, she turned to look.

There, in the corner of the kitchen, stood a tall man.

He was wearing a top hat, a long jacket and a white bow tie. Hilary knew that he was something from the past, from perhaps 100 years before. He didn't look at her, but walked straight past her and through the kitchen door. Then he disappeared.

Through walls
Many ghosts seem to be able to walk straight through walls and doors. This may be because the wall or door was not there when they were alive.

Computer ghost
In 1984 the ghost of a man called Harden sent messages through a computer. He wrote in old English, as it was used hundreds of years ago.

London Bridge
Engineers took down the old London Bridge over the Thames and rebuilt it in Arizona, USA. It is said that some of the bridge's ghosts went with it.

Hilary knew she had seen a ghost. The shadows and the cold spots had not been in her imagination. She looked around the kitchen, and her eyes stopped on the little china house. Everything had started after she had brought it back from England. She couldn't understand why a little china house could attract ghosts. But then, it was very old. Perhaps it had belonged to somebody who was now an unhappy ghost.

When her daughter Billie came to visit her, Hilary told her the story. Billie loved a good ghost story and was interested in the little china house. She decided to take it home with her.

Very soon, Billie noticed dark shadows moving across the walls. Something strange had entered her house.

One night, just after midnight, Billie lay in bed, thinking about the china house. She found that she was a little afraid.

But then she heard something that really frightened her. It was the sound of footsteps near her bedroom door. Very quietly, she got up and walked across the room. She paused for a second, then turned the door handle and looked out.

There, on the landing, was a tall man in old-fashioned clothes. Billie looked at the top hat, the long jacket and the white tie. He was exactly as her mother had described him. Billie opened her mouth to speak, or perhaps to scream. At that moment, the man disappeared.

Stop the clock
It is curious that many clocks have stopped working at the exact moment when their owners died.

Star mirror
Film star Marilyn Monroe is said to haunt a mirror that she owned. Marilyn died suddenly on 4 August, 1962.

Billie felt that the ghost was unhappy, but she didn't know why. Maybe it didn't like the stamps her mother had put in the little house.

The next morning, she phoned her mother and told her what had happened, and what she was going to do. She took the stamps out of the house and put in some money instead. But it didn't work. She knew this because the shadows continued to appear. Next, she tried some pens and pencils, but that didn't work either. She tried a number of different things, but there was no change in the feeling in her house.

In the end, she couldn't think of anything else to put into the little china house. She decided to leave it empty. Immediately, things improved. It was as if the sun had come out after the rain. There were no more dark shadows and her whole house felt warmer and happier. Billie knew that at last the ghost was happy, now that he had the little china house to himself.

Since then, Billie has not seen any more dark shadows. She hasn't seen the tall man in the top hat either. She still has the little china house. It's empty, of course. Or is it?

Many spices were sent from India to Europe and America. This was called the Spice Trade. Spices come from plants and are used for flavouring food. Cinnamon and ginger are spices.

Ginger root

Cinnamon sticks

Seaport
In the early 20th century, Bombay was one of the largest ports in India. Ships sailed from there to all parts of the world.

The last command

"Fire! Fire!" shouted the frightened seaman at the top of his voice. He ran up the ladder and appeared on the ship's deck. Behind him, a cloud of thick black smoke climbed into the air.

It was 1902 and the sailing ship *Firebird* was three days away from Bombay in India. A storm was coming, and the waves were growing bigger every hour. Down below the deck, an oil lamp had overturned, setting fire to some bags.

The men on deck moved quickly. Some ran to help those fighting the flames below. Others filled buckets with water to pass down to them. But it was no good. The fire moved with lightning speed through the ship. Men watched in horror as the mast itself caught light. Now it was only a matter of time.

"Lower all boats!" the captain shouted. "Get off the ship!"

As the crew rushed towards the boats, the mast broke into two pieces.

"Look out!" a man called, but nobody heard him above the noise of the flames. The falling mast hit the captain, and he dropped onto the deck, dead. Some of the men stopped running. Then one man broke from the crowd, took hold of the captain and moved him towards the side of the ship. Other men joined him, and together they got the captain into one of the boats. Pulling hard on the oars, they managed to get away from the ship. A few seconds later, the *Firebird* sank under the waves and disappeared.

Still sailing
In 1748, a British ship, the *Lady Lovibond*, hit the Goodwin Sands near Dover and sank. Every 50 years since then, people have seen the ghost of the ship in the area.

Three kilometres from the fire, another ship, the *James Gilbert*, was sailing away from the storm.

The young man at the wheel had turned his head to the side for a few minutes, watching some men who were working on the deck. When he looked to the front again, he saw a man in a captain's uniform standing there. The young man felt his heart miss a beat, because he had heard nobody come in.

The captain had a terrible cut on his head, and there was blood on his face.

"Change course to north-by-north-west," he said.

The young sailor knew that the new course would take the *James Gilbert* straight into the storm. However, it wasn't his place to argue. He hadn't realized there was another captain travelling with the ship, but that made no difference. He turned the wheel.

The captain of the *James Gilbert* was in his cabin. When he felt the ship change direction, he jumped up and ran for the nearest ladder.

"Why have you changed course?" he shouted, coming into the wheelhouse. "You're heading straight for the storm!"

The young man turned his head to look at the other captain. But there was nobody there.

"Are you mad, man? What came over you?" the captain shouted. Then he got himself under control. Explanations could wait. "Turn her back onto the previous course," he said.

At that moment, they heard a voice from high above. It was the lookout, calling from the top of the mast. "Boats! Straight ahead!"

Ghost ship
Many people have seen the famous ghost ship, the *Flying Dutchman*. On 11 July, 1881, the future king of Britain, George V, saw it in the South Atlantic when he was serving on *HMS Inconstant*.

A warning
While sailing to Britain on the *Waratah* in July 1909, Claude Sawyer had a dream in which a ghost told him the ship would sink. He changed ships and, shortly afterwards, the *Waratah* was lost at sea.

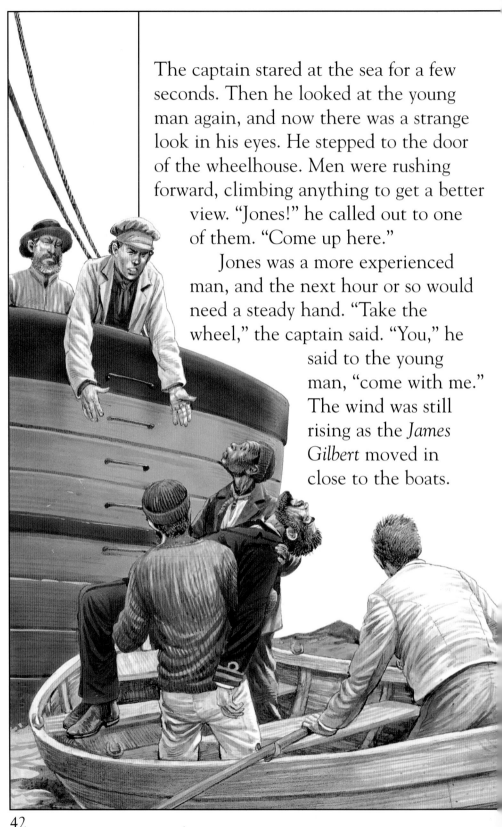

The captain stared at the sea for a few seconds. Then he looked at the young man again, and now there was a strange look in his eyes. He stepped to the door of the wheelhouse. Men were rushing forward, climbing anything to get a better view. "Jones!" he called out to one of them. "Come up here."

Jones was a more experienced man, and the next hour or so would need a steady hand. "Take the wheel," the captain said. "You," he said to the young man, "come with me." The wind was still rising as the *James Gilbert* moved in close to the boats.

Hands reached down from the ship and men climbed up onto her deck, happy to be safe. "It's very lucky you sailed this way," one of them said. "We thought we were all going to die in the storm."

The young man who had been in the wheelhouse stood above the last boat. "Will you help me with the captain," one of the sailors said. "He's dead." Between them, they got the body onto the ship.

As they laid the captain on the deck, his head fell to one side, showing a terrible cut and dried blood on his face. The young man stood up and took a step backwards. He stared at the dead man, lifting a hand to cover his eyes.

"What's wrong, boy?" asked the captain of the *James Gilbert*. "You look as if you've seen a ghost."

"I think I have," was the reply.

In broken sentences, he told his story. The men looked at the dead captain. They knew that he had saved their lives.

On the waves
In 1929, two dead crew members haunted the SS *Watertown*. The men's faces appeared on the waves. A crew member managed to take this photo.

Written request
A mysterious figure appeared on a British ship in 1828. He wrote "Sail north-west" on a blackboard, then disappeared. The captain obeyed the request and was able to save a ship and its crew that were stuck in ice.

What are ghosts?

Old ghosts
One of the first ghost stories ever written was *The Epic of Gilgamesh*. It was cut into stone more than 4,000 years ago.

Black dog
The most common type of reported ghost animal is a black dog.

For thousands of years, people have felt that ghosts are dead people who continue to move around in the world. Some may have a message for a friend or relative. Others may not be able to rest because they were murdered. Some seem to want to give a warning to the living – like Don Repo and the *Firebird's* captain.

Some ghosts repeat their actions. Roman soldiers walk through the cellars of a house in York, in the north of England. The house stands in the same place as where many soldiers used to live. The ghostly soldiers walk on the same level as the old Roman road, which is now about six metres below the modern house. When Ann Moberly and Eleanor Jourdain visited Versailles, they seemed to travel back in time. However, it may be that a moment in time, in October 1789, is endlessly repeating itself.

Most ghosts seem to haunt the places in which they lived when they were alive. In Brittany, France, the ghosts of the dead are said to return to their homes once a year, on 31 October, or Halloween. This date is associated with ghosts in many countries.

Ghost feelings
Some ghosts cannot be seen. Instead, they make people near them feel worried or sad.

Le Toussaint (*Halloween*), *from the magazine* L'Illustration (1895).

46   *Fake photograph of Jane Seymour, third wife of King Henry VIII of England.*

It does not often happen, but occasionally ghosts speak. Some people were skiing near Oslo, Norway, when a woman ordered them off her land. When she disappeared suddenly, they realized that a ghost had told them to go away.

Many people do not believe in ghosts. They think that anyone who says they have seen a ghost has too much imagination. They explain the "ghosts" as either tricks of the light, or something from inside the mind of the person who sees them. This is possible, but it is difficult to explain something that a number of people say they have seen at the same time.

Some ghosts are known to be tricks. This photograph is supposed to show the ghost of Jane Seymour, the third wife of the English king, Henry VIII. It was taken at the palace of Hampton Court near London. However, tests have shown that it isn't real.

Whatever we think about the subject, there are lots of contacts with ghosts that cannot easily be explained. In fact, the simplest explanation is probably that ghosts do exist. They may be all around you now – you just can't see them. Perhaps you should be grateful for that.

Ghostly smells
Some ghosts are connected with a smell. The headless ghost of a lady in Bovey House, England, always smells of flowers.

Ghost parties
On the Day of the Dead in Mexico, people invite the ghosts of dead friends and relatives to a party. They decorate the town with items like these wooden figures of skeletons.

Glossary

adventure
An unusual or exciting event that happens to somebody.

alarm
A bell or light that comes on to warn you of something.

automatic pilot
An instrument that keeps a plane flying without the pilot's help.

bowl
A deep plate that is used for holding soup.

bow tie
A man's tie that is tied in a bow.

to bury
To put a dead body, or something else, under the ground.

cabin
A room in a ship or an aeroplane.

captain
The person in charge of a ship or a plane.

cart
A vehicle with wheels that is pulled by a horse.

coach
A vehicle that people travel in. These used to be pulled by horses.

control tower
A high building at an airport, from where the planes are controlled.

crew
The people who work on a ship or an aeroplane.

deck
The floor on a ship.

to decorate
To make something look more attractive by painting it or fixing interesting or colourful things to it.

fairground
A fair is a travelling show that comes to a town perhaps once or twice every year. There are machines you can ride on and games you can play to win prizes. A fairground is the place where the fair happens.

footprints
The marks left by somebody's feet in snow, dust, mud, etc.

to haunt
When a ghost haunts a place, it appears there from time to time.

horror
This means great fear, often caused when you can't believe what is happening.

jawbone
The bone that is below the mouth.

journalist
A person who works on a newspaper, or in radio or TV, and helps to collect and write news stories.

lightbulb
The round glass part of an electric light.

lookout
The person on a ship who looks out for anything that might be dangerous.

mast
The long piece of wood that stands up on a ship and holds up the sails.

mechanic
A person who repairs and looks after engines.